KIDS ARE BABY GOATS

Kids Are Baby Goats

JANET CHIEFARI

Illustrated with photographs

DODD, MEAD & COMPANY : NEW YORK

599 1658

Library of Congress Cataloging in Publication Data

Chiefari, Janet.
  Kids are baby goats.

  Includes index.
  Summary: Traces the early life of Sunshine and
Samson, playful twin French Alpine goats born and
raised on a goat dairy farm.
  1. Kids (Goats)—Juvenile literature.   2. Goats—
Juvenile literature. [1. Goats.   2. Goats—Infancy]
I. Title.
SF383.35.C48   1984   636.3'907   83-25342
ISBN 0-396-08316-1

PICTURE CREDITS

Chewaucan Alpines, Lakeview, OR, 57; Gold Country Ranch, Placerville, CA (by Barbara Ingle), 51 (left); Ann Hagen Griffiths, 13, 14 (left), 22, 23, 27, 28, 32, 34, 37, 38, 39, 40, 41, 42, 43, 44, 55, 59; Idelmar Goat Dairy, Portage, WI (courtesy of Judy Kapture), 15; Khimaira Farm, Luray, VA (by Michael Brannon), 11, 50; *Times Record*, Troy, N.Y. (by Mike McMahon), 58. All other photographs are by Janet Chiefari.

For my children
PHILLIP, BOB, and AMY,
with love and appreciation for all
their help.

WHEN BABY GOATS PLAY, they run and jump and climb. They are lively, frisky animals, just full of energy. Interested in all that is around them, they look at and explore everything. They wag their tails like little puppies and always look happy.

Baby goats are called kids. Long ago, people noticed that children play a great deal like baby goats do. Perhaps that is why children are often called *kids*.

Goat kids can be found on farms and dairies throughout the United States. Many children have seen them at game farms or in a zoo. Some may even have had the chance to touch their fluffy, soft fur at petting zoos or local fairs.

Eight-year-old Amy is a lucky girl. She can touch and play with goat kids any time. Amy lives on a goat dairy.

Goat dairies, like cow dairies, are in the business of producing and selling milk. The female goat is called a doe. The male goat is called a buck. The does at a dairy produce about one gallon of creamy, white milk each day. It tastes good and is very similar to cow's milk. Many people drink goat's milk because they are allergic to cow's milk. Also, cheeses are made from goat's milk.

Buck

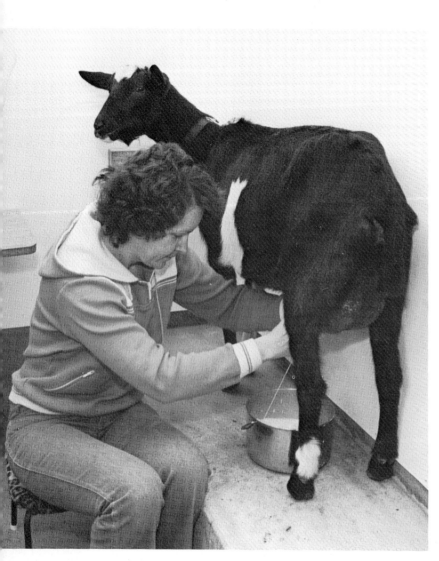

Doe

Many goat dairies are small with only eight or ten goats. The does are milked by hand.

Larger dairies use milking machines and may have 200 to 300 milking does.

The dairy doe must give birth to kids every year in order to produce milk. Most does have two kids or twins. Single, triplet (3), quadruplet (4), or even quintuplet (5) kids also occur.

The doe and buck usually mate in the fall. Then the baby goat develops inside the mother for five months. In the springtime, the pregnant doe gives birth to her kids in a special room called a kidding pen. It is a clean place where she can be quiet and away from the other animals. People who work at the dairy are with her to help if necessary.

When the baby goat is born, the doe quickly licks its face with her tongue. This is to clear the kid's nose and mouth so it can breathe.

She continues to lick the baby's wet fur to clean and warm it.

She talks to her baby with a soft, grunting sound as she licks it. The kid starts to bleat loudly, "Maaa, maaa."

Then another kid is born. The first was a buck. It is a doe this time.

Both kids are miniatures of their parents. Each one weighs about seven pounds. Their eyes are open wide and they can see everything around them.

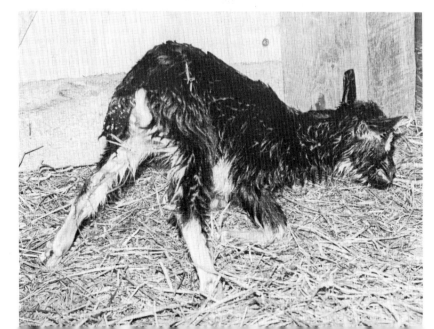

Within minutes they struggle to their feet. Their legs are wobbly, but they soon manage to find that first meal from their mother's udder.

The doe's udder has two teats or nipples, not four like the cow's. The baby goats suck colostrum (co-los-trum) from the teats. Colostrum is a thick, yellow liquid. It has antibodies and nutrients which the kids need for the first two or three days of life. Then the doe will produce milk for them to drink.

At the dairy where Amy lives, many kids are born each spring. Sunshine and Samson are twin goat kids that were born there one bright morning in March. Samson is a buck and Sunshine is a doe. They are French Alpine goats.

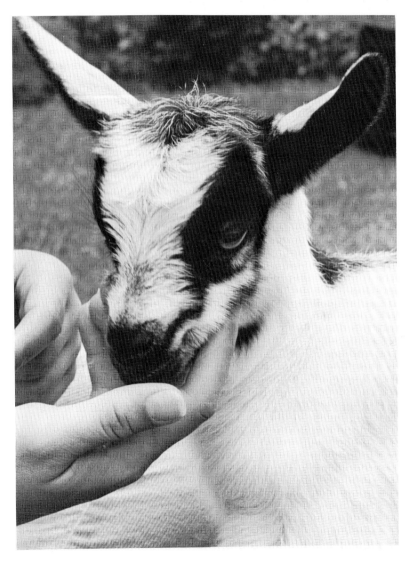

French Alpine goats have ears that stand up straight. They can turn their ears in the direction of a sound to listen.

French Alpines come in many colors and combinations of colors. Samson is called a *cou blanc* because he has a white neck and black hindquarters. Sunshine is a *chamoisee* (sham-wah-zay). This means that she is brown with black markings on her face and back.

On the dairy there are two other breeds or
kinds of dairy goats and their kids—Saanen
goats and Toggenburg goats. Saanens are
always pure white.

Toggenburgs are always light brown with white markings on their faces and legs. Except for their colors, they look much like the French Alpines.

Sunshine, Samson, and all the other kids
at the dairy live in pens designed for their
special care. To tell the kids apart, each one
is named and given a tattoo or number in its
ear soon after birth.

Three or four times a day each kid is fed milk from a bottle with a nipple. They are petted and held. The kids get a lot of love and attention from Amy and her family. They learn to trust people to meet their needs and to care for them gently.

From the time that Sunshine and Samson are just a few days old, they begin to play a fighting game. They butt or hit their foreheads together and then push one another back and forth. This does not hurt them. It is a way of testing their strength.

The one who is the stronger becomes the leader. As adult goats, this will no longer be a game but a serious matter. An order of strength, going from weakest to strongest, is established in every herd or group of goats.

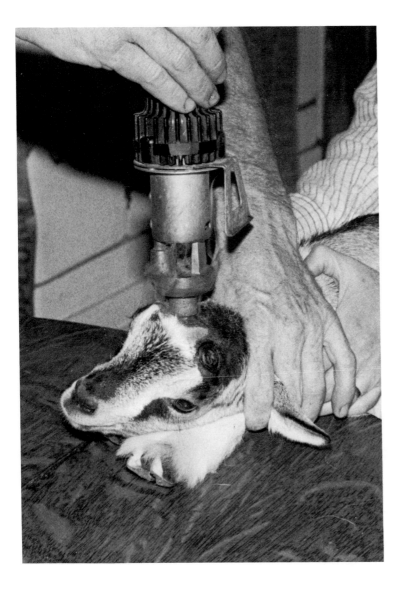

When Sunshine and Samson are about one week of age, they have their horns removed. This is called disbudding. A hot iron is applied to the horn spot—the place where the horn has just started to grow. It destroys the horn cells.

Although this is uncomfortable for a minute, it may save their lives later. Goat horns grow quite long and they are pointed at the ends. The horns can get caught in fences or hay mangers, seriously hurting the animals. Also, goats can hurt one another with their sharp horns.

The disbudding leaves round, dark spots on their heads. Hair soon grows over these spots.

Some goats never grow horns. They are called polled goats and can be any breed.

As the kids at the dairy get a little older and stronger, they are fed their milk from a lambar. A lambar is a feeding device which allows many kids to nurse from one bucket of milk. The kids suck on nipples which are placed in holes around the top of a bucket. A tube attached to each nipple reaches down into the milk. It is like sucking milk through a straw. Wagging their tails rapidly, they nurse until the last drop of milk is gone.

After two or three weeks, the goat kids start to eat hay or dried grasses and grain. The grain is a mixture of corn, oats, and wheat. They also begin to nibble on grasses in the pasture.

A goat's teeth are perfectly designed to tear off grasses, leaves from brush-type plants, and even to scrape bark from trees. The kids have eight small, sharp teeth in their lower front jaw. These teeth meet a hard pad in the upper jaw. Goats do not have any upper front teeth. They do have 24 molars—large chewing or grinding teeth—on the top and bottom in the back of their mouths. Like children, their baby teeth fall out and are replaced by permanent teeth.

Do goat kids bite people with their sharp teeth? No! They may suck at fingers or even noses, or tickle petting hands with their lips, but they do not bite. Kids are very gentle animals.

Kids will rarely eat anything that is dirty or bad for them. The older goats teach the younger ones to avoid poisonous weeds in the pasture. Most people believe that goats will eat anything, but this is not true. They are curious animals and will *feel* everything with their sensitive lips, but they will not eat it unless it tastes like good, clean food.

Samson and Sunshine eat well and grow quickly. By the time they are three months old, each weighs almost 40 pounds. The soft, fluffy fur has become sleek and silky. Their noses are longer and thinner. Like most *chamoisees*, Sunshine's color has darkened.

They do not drink milk anymore but eat hay, grain, and grass as the adult goats do.

All the kids spend less time sleeping now. Sometimes they lie or stand quietly and *chew*. It looks almost as if they were chewing gum.

This is because goats are ruminants or cud-chewing animals. When goats eat, they only chew their food a little bit before they swallow it. When they are resting later, a small amount of food, called a cud, is returned to the mouth. This time, they chew it very thoroughly before swallowing it again.

The eyes of Samson and Sunshine look different from those of other animals. This is because the pupil in a goat's eye has a rectangular shape instead of being round.

Samson's wattles—the little round balls of fur on his neck close to his chin—are now easy to see. All goats do not have wattles. They are a decorative feature that some does and bucks inherit from their parents.

... follow the leader ...

If kids are not sleeping, eating, or chewing their cud, they are playing! They play games like king of the mountain...

…and tag.

Climbing on *anything* is terrific fun! They
will take any challenge—even when it's a
long way back down. They are very sure-
footed.

Jumping! Kids do not walk when they play, they bounce from place to place. They leap up into the air, spinning and twisting. They jump over, on top of, and off of everything. Sometimes they seem to think they can fly.

When children jump and play, they need shoes to protect their feet from the stony, rough ground. Goat kids have hoofs to protect theirs. A goat's hoofs are cloven, or in two parts, like those of a cow or deer. They are like a very thick fingernail. They grow long and must be cut so that the kids can stand flat or squarely on their hoofs. Then their feet and legs will grow properly.

Samson and the other kids have their hoofs cut at least once a month.

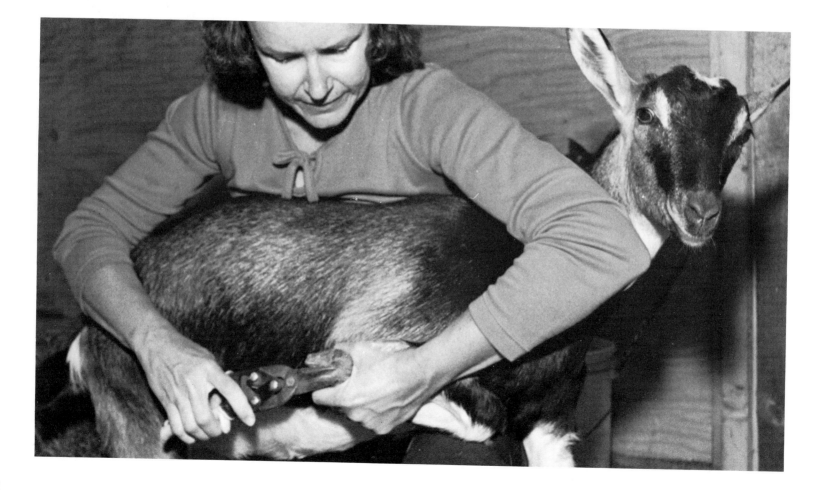

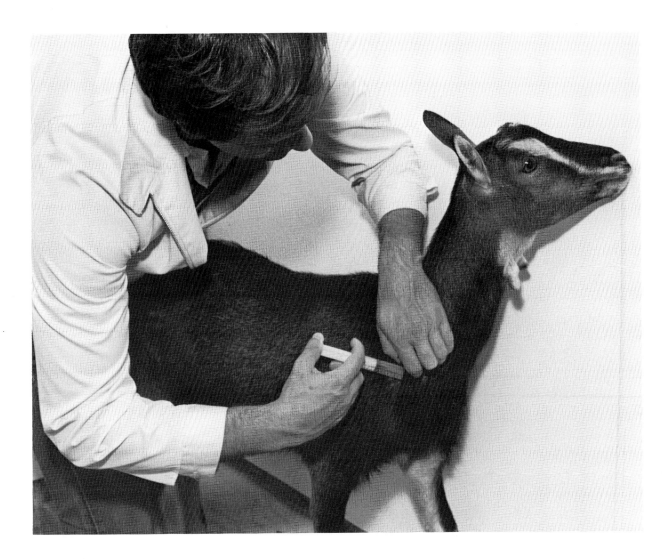

Goat kids also need other regular health care. They have check-ups by a doctor called a veterinarian. He examines them to be sure they are strong and growing well. He also gives them shots. Goat kids need protection against diseases such as tetanus, just as children do.

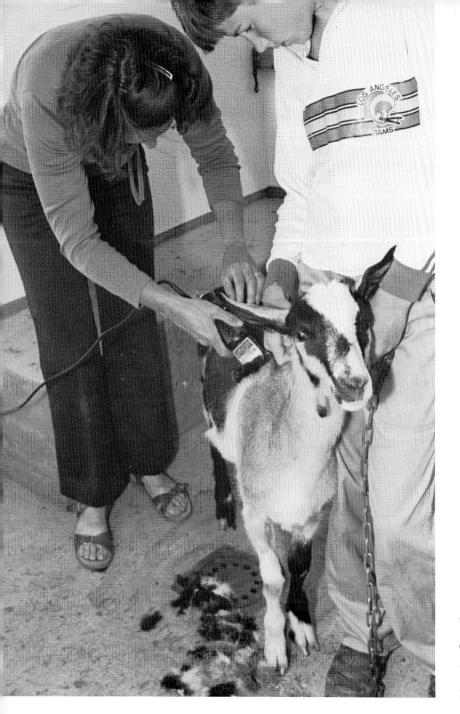

Kids get hair cuts too. This is usually done with electric clippers. All of their hair is clipped to $1/4''$ to $1/2''$ in length. This keeps them cool and clean during the hot summer months.

Clipping is often required when the kids are going to be entered in a goat show or competition. Large and small competitions are held in areas throughout the country every year. Goats from farms and dairies can compete at any age. The kids are judged against other goat kids of the same sex, age, and breed.

Sunshine's first show is at the county fair late in the summer. To prepare for the competition, Amy practiced leading and posing Sunshine for many hours. Most of the children participating learned how to handle and show their kids in 4-H Clubs. Other children, like Amy, who are too young for 4-H, were taught by their parents or older brothers and sisters.

Amy walks Sunshine slowly around in a large circle in the show-ring. Several other children lead their kids around with her. The judge looks the six-month-old does over carefully. Then she selects kids for first, second, and third place. She decides that these goats best meet the standards for their breed and age. The winners receive ribbons for an award.

Amy and Sunshine are very happy at being
a part of this game. Amy is proud of her kid
as she receives a ribbon for first place.
Sunshine loves the petting and attention.

But next time, Amy must be more careful where she places her ribbon. Sunshine's nibbling goat lips just have to find out if it is anything good to eat!

Amy also discovers that competitions are a great way to get to see all of the different breeds of dairy goats. Alpines, Saanens, and Toggenburgs like the ones at the dairy are there. And it is an added treat to see Nubian, Oberhasli, and LaMancha kids.

Nubian goats have long, wide, hanging ears that frame their faces. Nubians are the most popular breed of dairy goat in the United States. They come in many colors. Some are even polkadotted!

Their voices sound different from all the other goats. They sound like babies crying.

Where are his ears? The LaMancha has such small ears, they are hard to find. This makes him look very different from the other goats, but he can hear just as well. LaManchas may be black, white, brown, or a mixture of colors.

The Oberhasli is a Swiss dairy goat. They
have ears like the French Alpines. They are a
distinctive brownish-red outlined in black.

Amy meets a boy who brought his two-day-old Oberhasli kid to the fair.

After the great activity and excitement of the show, Amy and Sunshine are glad to be back home. For the next few days, they spend their time together walking through fields near the dairy.

Sunshine, Samson, and several of the other kids walk along beside Amy just as a dog would do. They follow her wherever she goes. One kid may stop to nibble at a tasty plant and then run as fast as it can to catch up with the rest. Sometimes they all dart ahead for a quick race and then race back to her again.

They all love this walking adventure game.

The fall days grow shorter and colder, and
when the snow covers the pastures, the goats
stay in the barn all the time. Goats do not
like to get their feet wet!

The kids eat and grow rapidly throughout the quiet winter months. By spring, the one-year-old goats are no longer kids but full-grown animals.

Samson has become strong and muscular. He is much larger than Sunshine now. Like all bucks, he has grown a handsome, long beard. Samson is to be sold to another dairy as a herd sire, or father, of their goat kids.

Sunshine weighs over 100 pounds now and stands 32" high. She is a beautiful, gentle animal that enjoys people, and people truly enjoy her. Sunshine is soon to have a kid of her own.

When Sunshine's kidding day arrives, she gives birth to a beautiful little buck. Then she proudly joins the line of does producing delicious milk for the dairy's customers.

One morning as Amy is milking Sunshine, she thinks about how tiny the goat was just a short while ago. She remembers the long walks she and the kid shared and the games they played together.

"Sunshine grew up too fast," Amy says to her mom.

"She sure did," her mother answers, "but now she will be giving you brand-new kids to play with every year."

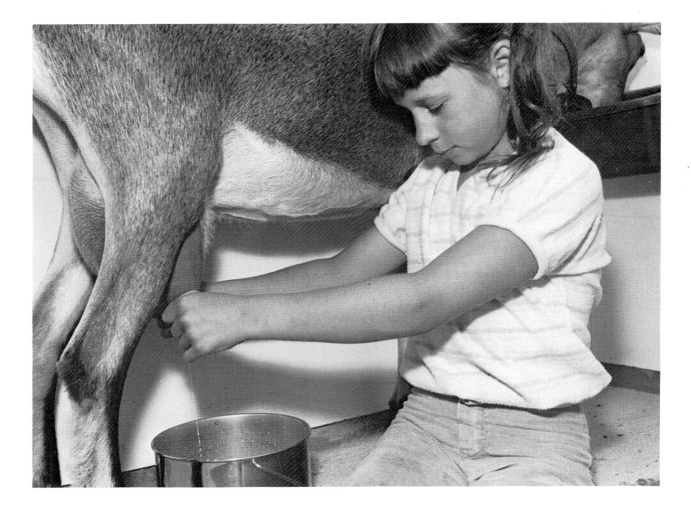

INDEX